CROCK·POT®
◆ THE ORIGINAL SLOW COOKER ◆

SOUPS & STEWS

Publications International, Ltd.

© 2008 Publications International, Ltd.
All recipe photographs © 2008 Publications International, Ltd.

All rights reserved. This publication may not be reproduced or quoted in whole or in part by any means whatsoever without written permission from:

Louis Weber, CEO
Publications International, Ltd.
7373 North Cicero Avenue
Lincolnwood, IL 60712

Permission is never granted for commercial purposes.

Material on pages 4-5, 7-9, 11, 12, 14, 16, 18, 20, 22, 28, 31, 32, 34, 36, 38, 40, 42, 46, 47, 49, 51, 52, 54, 56, 62-65, 67, 68, 70, 74, 78, 79, 81, 83, 84, 86, 88, 92 and 93 © Sunbeam Products, Inc. doing business as Jarden Consumer Solutions. All rights reserved. All other material and recipes © Publications International, Ltd.

CROCK-POT® and the **CROCK-POT®** logo
are registered trademarks of Sunbeam Products, Inc. used under license.

Recipes on pages 7-9, 11, 12, 14, 16, 31, 34, 36, 51, 52, 54, 56, 63, 65, 67, 68, 70, 78, 83, 84, 86 and 88 developed by Amy Golino.

Photograph on page 6 © Corbis. Front cover photography and photography on pages 10, 15, 17, 30, 33, 35, 37, 50, 53, 55, 57, 66, 69, 71, 85, 87 and 89 by Stephen Hamilton Photographics, Inc.

Photography: Stephen Hamilton Photographics, Inc.
Photographers: Tate Hunt, Jennifer Marx and Brian Wetzstein
Photographers' Assistants: Rochelle Russo and Christy Clow
Prop Stylist: Tom Hamilton
Food Stylists: Donna Coates, Kim Hartman and Cindy Melin
Assistant Food Stylists: Breana Moeller and Sheila Granner

Pictured on the front cover: Northwest Beef and Vegetable Soup *(page 20)*.

Pictured on the back cover (clockwise from top): Spring Pea and Mint Broth Soup *(page 88)*, Orange Soup *(page 86)* and Corn Chowder with Basil Oil *(page 83)*.

ISBN-13: 978-1-4127-2833-1
ISBN-10: 1-4127-2833-9

Manufactured in China.

8 7 6 5 4 3 2 1

table of contents

- **4** Slow Cooker Hints and Tips
- **6** Basic Stocks
- **10** Beef and Lamb
- **30** Chicken and Turkey
- **50** Pork, Ham and Sausage
- **66** Seafood
- **82** Vegetable
- **94** Index
- **96** Metric Conversion Chart

introduction

Slow Cooker Hints and Tips

Slow Cooker Sizes

Smaller slow cookers, such as 1- to 3½-quart models, are the perfect size for singles, a couple, empty-nesters and also for serving dips. Try Beef, Lentil and Onion Soup on page 27 in a smaller model slow cooker.

While medium-size slow cookers (those holding somewhere between 3 quarts and 5 quarts) will easily cook enough food at a time to feed a small family, they are also convenient for holiday side dishes or appetizers. There are several great recipes for medium-size slow cookers in this book, such as Thai-Style Chicken and Pumpkin Soup on page 49 and Spring Pea and Mint Broth Soup on page 88.

Large slow cookers are great for large family dinners, holiday entertaining and potluck suppers. A 6- to 7-quart model is ideal if you like to make meals in advance and have dinner tonight and store leftovers for another day. The Chicken Miso Soup with Shiitake Mushrooms on page 31 is perfect for feeding a crowd.

Types of Slow Cookers

Current models of **CROCK-POT**® slow cookers come equipped with many different features and benefits, from auto cook programs, to stovetop-safe stoneware to timed programming. Visit **www.crockpot.com** to find the slow cooker that best suits your needs and lifestyle.

Cooking, Stirring, and Food Safety

CROCK-POT® slow cookers are safe to leave unattended. The outer heating base may get hot as it cooks, but it should not pose a fire hazard. The heating element in the heating base functions at a low wattage and is safe for your countertops.

Your slow cooker should be filled about ½- to ¾-full for most recipes unless otherwise instructed. Lean meats such as chicken or pork tenderloin will cook faster than meats with more connective tissue and fat such as beef chuck or pork shoulder. Bone-in meats will take longer than boneless cuts. Typical slow cooker dishes take approximately 7 to 8 hours to reach the simmer point on LOW and about 3 to 4 hours on HIGH. Once the vegetables and meat start to simmer and braise, their flavors will fully blend and meat will become fall-off-the-bone tender.

According to the USDA, all bacteria are killed at a temperature of 165°F. It is important to follow the recommended cooking times and not to remove the lid often, especially early in the cooking process when heat is building up inside the unit. If you need to remove the lid to check on your food or are adding additional ingredients, remember to allow additional cooking time to ensure food is cooked through and tender.

Large slow cookers, the 6- to 7-quart sizes, may benefit from a quick stir halfway during the cook time to help distribute heat and promote even cooking. It is usually unnecessary to stir at all as even ½ cup liquid will help to distribute heat, and the crockery is the perfect medium for holding food at an even temperature throughout the cooking process.

Oven-Safe

All **CROCK-POT**® slow cooker removable crockery inserts may (without their lids) be used in ovens at up to 400°F safely. Also, all **CROCK-POT**® slow cookers are microwavable without their lids. If you own another brand slow cooker, please refer to your owner's manual for specific crockery cooking-medium tolerances.

Frozen Food

Frozen food or partially frozen food can be successfully cooked in a slow cooker; however, it will require longer cooking than the same recipe made with fresh food. Using an instant-read thermometer is recommended to ensure meat is fully cooked.

Pasta and Rice

If you are converting a stovetop recipe to be made in a slow cooker and the recipe calls for uncooked pasta, cook it on the stovetop just until slightly tender before adding to slow cooker. If you are converting a recipe that calls for cooked rice, stir in raw rice with the other ingredients; add ¼ cup extra liquid per ¼ cup of raw rice.

Beans

Beans must be softened completely before combining with sugar and/or acidic foods. Sugar and acid have a hardening effect on beans and will prevent softening. Fully cooked canned beans may be used as a substitute for dried beans.

Vegetables

Root vegetables often cook more slowly than meat. Cut vegetables accordingly to cook at the same rate as meat, large or small, or lean versus marbled, and place near the sides or bottom of the stoneware to facilitate cooking.

Herbs

Fresh herbs add flavor and color when added at the end of the cooking cycle, but for dishes with shorter cook times, hearty, fresh herbs such as rosemary and thyme hold up well. If added at the beginning, many fresh herbs' flavor will dissipate over long cook times.

Ground and/or dried herbs and spices work well in slow cooking and may be added at beginning. The flavor power of all herbs and spices can vary greatly depending on their particular strength and shelf life. Use chili powders and garlic powder sparingly as these can sometimes intensify over the long cook times. Always taste the dish before serving and adjust seasonings, including salt and pepper.

Liquids

Excess liquid can be cooked down and concentrated after slow cooking on the stovetop or by removing the meat and vegetables from the **CROCK-POT®** slow cooker, stirring in cornstarch or tapioca and setting the slow cooker to HIGH. Cook on HIGH about 15 minutes or until juices are thickened.

Milk

Milk, cream, and sour cream break down during extended cooking. When possible, add them during last the 15 to 30 minutes of cooking, until just heated through.

Fish

Fish is delicate and should be stirred in gently during the last 15 to 30 minutes of cooking time. Cook until just cooked through and serve immediately.

basic stocks

Slow Cooker Vegetable Stock

1. Add all ingredients to 6- to 7-quart **CROCK-POT**® slow cooker and fill three-quarters full with water. Season with salt. Cook on HIGH 6 to 8 hours or on LOW 10 to 12 hours.

2. Strain stock and discard solids. Allow stock to cool to room temperature and refrigerate, freeze or use immediately.

Note: *This recipe calls for bay leaves, thyme and parsley, but any combination of herbs and spices can be used to create a signature broth for a special soup such as Vietnamese Pho. Try a variety of classic herbs and spices such as rosemary, sage, parsley and chives, or experiment with more exotic varieties such as Thai basil, mint, cilantro, ginger, lemongrass and star anise. Varying the vegetables to suit the soup also offers limitless possibilities with additions such as turnip, sweet potato, yam, rutabaga, celery root, fennel and mushrooms.*

3 **carrots, coarsely chopped**
3 **parsnips, coarsely chopped**
3 **onions, quartered**
3 **leeks, coarsely chopped**
3 **stalks celery, coarsely chopped**
3 **bay leaves**
2 **sprigs thyme**
4 **sprigs parsley**
8 **whole peppercorns**
　Water
　Kosher salt, to taste

Makes 10 to 12 cups stock

basic stocks

Slow Cooker Beef or Veal Stock

- 3 to 4 tablespoons vegetable oil, divided
- 3 to 4 pounds beef or veal bones, preferably marrow or knuckle bones
- 9 cups water, divided
- 2 large leeks, thoroughly cleaned, cut into 1-inch pieces
- 3 carrots, cut into 1-inch pieces
- 3 cups onions, coarsely chopped
- 2 stalks celery, cut into 1-inch pieces
- 1 tablespoon tomato paste
- 2 fresh thyme sprigs
- 2 large sprigs fresh flat-leaf parsley
- 1 bay leaf
- ½ tablespoon black peppercorns

1. Preheat oven to 450°F. Coat large roasting pan with 1 to 2 tablespoons oil. Arrange bones in single layer in pan and roast in middle of oven, turning once or twice, until browned, 30 to 45 minutes.

2. Using tongs, transfer bones to a 6- to 7-quart **CROCK-POT**® slow cooker. Add 8 cups water. Discard fat from roasting pan, and add ½ cup water to roasting pan, stirring and scraping up brown bits; add to **CROCK-POT**® slow cooker. Cook on HIGH 5 to 6 hours or on LOW 8 to 10 hours.

3. In last hour of slow cooking bones, preheat oven to 450°F. Coat roasting pan with remaining 1 to 2 tablespoons oil and arrange leeks, carrots, onions and celery in single layer. Roast in middle of oven, stirring once or twice, until golden brown, 20 to 30 minutes. Transfer vegetables to **CROCK-POT**® slow cooker and immediately add remaining ½ cup water to hot pan, stirring and scraping up brown bits, then add to **CROCK-POT**® slow cooker. Add tomato paste, thyme, parsley, bay leaf and peppercorns; cook on HIGH 2 hours more.

4. Remove bones with tongs and discard. Pour stock in batches through large sieve into stockpot and discard solids. Allow stock to cool to room temperature and place in refrigerator overnight. Before using or freezing, discard any fat that rises to top of chilled stock.

Note: *To quickly cool down stock for safe refrigerator storage, pour strained stock into a stockpot and place in a sink or large bowl of ice, stirring often.*

Makes 8 to 10 cups stock

Slow Cooker Chicken Stock

1. Place all ingredients in 6- to 7-quart **CROCK-POT**® slow cooker and add enough water to fill three-quarters full. Cook 8 hours on HIGH or 12 hours on LOW.

2. Strain out solids, cool and refrigerate 12 hours. Skim off and discard any fat on top of stock and use as desired.

- 1 large chicken (4 to 6 pounds), cut into pieces
- 1 package (16 ounces) celery, cut into large chunks
- 1 large carrot, peeled and cut into 2- to 3-inch pieces
- 2 onions or leeks, quartered
- 2 large parsnips, peeled and coarsely chopped
- ½ cup loosely packed fresh herbs such as flat-leaf parsley, dill, thyme, chervil or a combination
- Kosher salt and black pepper, to taste

Makes about 10 cups stock

Slow Cooker Fish Stock

1. Heat olive oil in skillet over medium-high heat. Add onion, carrots and celery. Cook until tender and lightly browned, 6 to 8 minutes. Add wine and scrape browned bits off bottom of pan. Pour mixture into 5- to 7-quart **CROCK-POT**® slow cooker. Stir in remaining ingredients and cook on HIGH 3½ hours.

2. Skim off any foam; strain and let cool. Chill stock in refrigerator and remove fat that rises to surface.

- 2 tablespoons olive oil
- 1 large onion, chopped
- 2 carrots, chopped
- 2 stalks celery, chopped
- 1 cup white wine
- 2 whole tilapia, scaled and gutted
- 8 cups water
- 1 sprig thyme
- 4 sprigs parsley
- 4 whole black peppercorns
- 2 teaspoons salt

Makes about 8 cups stock

beef and lamb

Sweet and Sour Moroccan Lamb Soup

1. Heat olive oil in heavy pan over medium-high to high heat. Sear meat on all sides.

2. Place meat in 4½- to 6-quart **CROCK-POT®** slow cooker and add ginger, turmeric, tomatoes, water, onion, cilantro, salt and pepper. Cook on HIGH 8 hours or on LOW 12 hours.

3. Add cooked orzo, lemon juice and cinnamon. Taste and adjust seasonings. Ladle into serving bowls and garnish with chopped dates.

Makes 4 to 6 servings

3 tablespoons olive oil

1 pound boneless lamb shoulder, cut into thin strips, fat removed

1 teaspoon peeled and grated ginger

½ teaspoon ground turmeric

1 can (28 ounces) peeled plum tomatoes, drained

7 cups cold water

1 large onion, chopped

1 bunch fresh cilantro, stemmed, ¼ cup loosely packed reserved for garnish

Kosher salt and black pepper

1 cup orzo, cooked

2 tablespoons lemon juice

½ teaspoon ground cinnamon

1 cup dates, finely chopped

beef and lamb

Mushroom Soup

- 2 tablespoons olive oil
- 2 large Vidalia onions, coarsely chopped
- 1 package (10 ounces) cremini mushrooms
- 1 package (10 ounces) button mushrooms
- Kosher salt and black pepper
- 2 tablespoons butter
- 6 to 10 cloves garlic, peeled and coarsely chopped
- 2 tablespoons sherry
- 4 cups Slow Cooker Beef Stock

1. Heat olive oil in large skillet over medium-high heat. Add onions and mushrooms and season well with salt and pepper. Cook vegetables, stirring often, until cooked down and fragrant, about 8 to 10 minutes.

2. Add butter and garlic and cook gently another 1 to 2 minutes. Add sherry to pan and stir to scrape up any bits stuck to bottom.

3. Transfer sherry and vegetables into 2½- to 5-quart **CROCK-POT®** slow cooker and add stock. Cover and cook on HIGH 3 to 4 hours or on LOW 5 to 6 hours.

Note: Mushroom soup is usually made with beef stock because the deep flavor of the mushrooms balances perfectly with a hearty stock. Try experimenting with a variety of mushrooms, but don't use wild mushrooms only. Although they add great flavor, they can be too intense if used exclusively.

Makes 4 to 6 servings

beef and lamb

Hot Pot Noodle Soup

2 to 3 tablespoons peanut oil
2 large onions, chopped
1 large carrot, peeled and chopped
3 stalks lemongrass, thinly sliced
⅔ cup peeled and minced fresh ginger
8 garlic cloves, peeled and minced
7 whole star anise
3 quarts (12 cups) Slow Cooker Beef Stock
3 tablespoons fish sauce (nam pla)*
1 package (12 ounces) fresh udon noodles or fresh linguine
1 tablespoon sesame oil
3 cups bean sprouts
4 green onions, thinly sliced
4 serrano chiles, thinly sliced
6 tablespoons chopped fresh basil
6 tablespoons chopped fresh mint
6 tablespoons chopped fresh cilantro
Lime wedges for serving

*Nam pla, Vietnamese fish sauce, can be found in the ethnic section of many grocery stores and in Asian markets.

1. Heat peanut oil in heavy large pot over medium-high heat. Add onions, carrot, lemongrass, ginger, garlic and star anise. Cook, stirring, until vegetables are softened. Transfer mixture to 6- to 7-quart **CROCK-POT®** slow cooker. Add stock and fish sauce. Cover and cook on HIGH 4 to 5 hours or on LOW 7 to 9 hours. Remove star anise. Taste and adjust seasonings as desired.

2. Cook noodles in large pot of boiling salted water until tender. Drain; rinse under cold water. Return to same pot. Toss noodles with sesame oil.

3. To serve, place noodles in individual bowls, top with bean sprouts, green onions, chiles, basil, mint and cilantro. Ladle soup over noodles and serve with lime wedges.

Tip: Try this with pork, chicken or seafood, infusing the appropriate stock with the aromatic herbs and spices.

Makes 6 to 8 servings

beef and lamb

Chuck and Stout Soup

- 2 tablespoons olive oil
- 3 pounds beef chuck, cut into 1-inch cubes
- Kosher salt and black pepper
- 8 cups Slow Cooker Beef Stock
- 3 large onions, thinly sliced
- 3 stalks celery, diced
- 6 carrots, peeled and diced
- 4 cloves garlic, peeled and minced
- 2 packages (10 ounces each) cremini mushrooms, thinly sliced
- 1 package (about 1 ounce) dried porcini mushrooms, processed to a fine powder
- 4 sprigs fresh thyme
- 1 bottle (12 ounces) stout beer
- Flat-leaf parsley to garnish

1. Heat oil in skillet over medium-high to high heat. Season meat with salt and pepper. In two batches, brown beef on all sides, taking care to not crowd meat. Meanwhile, in large saucepan, bring beef stock to a boil and reduce by half.

2. Remove beef and place in 6- to 7-quart **CROCK-POT®** slow cooker. Add reduced stock and remaining ingredients (except parsley) and cook on HIGH 6 hours or on LOW 10 hours.

3. Garnish with parsley and serve.

Note: *A coffee grinder works best for processing dried mushrooms, but a food processor or blender can also be used.*

Makes 6 to 8 servings

beef and lamb

Caramelized French Onion Soup

- 4 large sweet onions, peeled
- 4 tablespoons (½ stick) butter
- 2 cups dry white wine
- 8 cups Slow Cooker Beef Stock
- 2 cups water
- 1 tablespoon minced fresh thyme
- 6 large seasoned croutons
- 1 cup Swiss or Gruyère cheese, shredded

1. Cut each onion into quarters. Cut each quarter into ¼-inch-thick slices. Heat skillet over medium heat until hot. Add butter and onions. Cook, stirring every 7 to 8 minutes. Transfer to 4½-quart **CROCK-POT®** slow cooker when onions are soft and caramelized, about 45 to 50 minutes.

2. Add wine to skillet and let liquid reduce to about ½ cup, simmering about 15 minutes. Transfer to **CROCK-POT®** slow cooker.

3. Add stock, water and thyme to **CROCK-POT®** slow cooker. Cover; cook on HIGH 2½ hours or until thoroughly heated.

4. To serve, ladle soup into individual ovenproof soup bowls. Place 1 crouton on top of each, and sprinkle cheese over crouton. Preheat oven broiler and place bowls on top shelf of oven. Broil 3 to 5 minutes or until cheese is melted and golden. Serve immediately.

Makes 6 servings

beef and lamb

Northwest Beef and Vegetable Soup

- 2 tablespoons olive oil
- 1 pound lean stew beef, fat removed and cut into 1-inch cubes
- 1 medium onion, chopped
- 1 clove garlic, minced
- 3½ cups canned crushed tomatoes, undrained
- 1 can (15 ounces) white beans, drained and rinsed
- 1 buttercup squash, peeled and diced
- 1 turnip, peeled and diced
- 1 large potato, peeled and diced
- 2 stalks celery, sliced
- 2 tablespoons minced fresh basil
- 1½ teaspoons salt
- 1 teaspoon black pepper
- 8 cups water

1. Heat oil in skillet over medium heat until hot. Sear beef on all sides, turning as it browns. Add onion and garlic during last few minutes of searing. Transfer to 4½-quart **CROCK-POT®** slow cooker.

2. Add remaining ingredients. Gently stir well to combine. Cover; cook on HIGH 2 hours. Turn **CROCK-POT®** slow cooker to LOW. Cook 4 to 6 hours longer. Stir occasionally and adjust seasonings to taste.

Makes 6 to 8 servings

beef and lamb

Wild Mushroom Beef Stew

1½ to 2 pounds beef stew meat, cut into 1-inch cubes
2 tablespoons all-purpose flour
½ teaspoon salt
½ teaspoon black pepper
1½ cups Slow Cooker Beef Stock
1 teaspoon Worcestershire sauce
1 clove garlic, minced
1 bay leaf
1 teaspoon paprika
4 shiitake mushrooms, sliced
2 medium carrots, sliced
2 medium potatoes, diced
1 small white onion, chopped
1 stalk celery, sliced

1. Put beef in 3½- to 4½-quart **CROCK-POT®** slow cooker. Mix together flour, salt and pepper and sprinkle over meat; stir to coat each piece of meat with flour. Add remaining ingredients and stir to mix well.

2. Cover; cook on HIGH 4 to 6 hours or on LOW 10 to 12 hours. Stir before serving.

Note: *This classic beef stew is given a twist with the addition of flavorful shiitake mushrooms. If shiitake mushrooms are unavailable in your local grocery store, you can substitute other mushrooms of your choice. For extra punch, add a few dried porcini mushrooms to the stew.*

Tip: *You may double the amount of meat, mushrooms, carrots, potatoes, onion and celery for the 5-, 6- or 7-quart* **CROCK-POT®** *slow cooker.*

Makes 5 servings

beef and lamb

Italian Beef and Barley Soup

- 1 boneless beef top sirloin steak (about 1½ pounds)
- 1 tablespoon vegetable oil
- 4 medium carrots or parsnips, cut into ¼-inch slices
- 1 cup chopped onion
- 1 teaspoon dried thyme
- ½ teaspoon dried rosemary
- ¼ teaspoon black pepper
- ⅓ cup uncooked pearl barley
- 3 to 4 cups Slow Cooker Beef Stock
- 1 can (about 14 ounces) diced tomatoes with Italian seasoning, undrained

1. Cut beef into 1-inch pieces. Heat oil over medium-high heat in large skillet. Brown beef on all sides; set aside.

2. Place carrots and onion in 3½- to 4½-quart **CROCK-POT®** slow cooker; sprinkle with thyme, rosemary and pepper. Top with barley and beef. Pour stock and tomatoes over meat.

3. Cover; cook on LOW 8 to 10 hours or until beef is tender.

Tip: *Choose pearl barley rather than quick-cooking barley; it will stand up to long cooking.*

Makes 6 servings

beef and lamb

Lamb Stew

- 1 large onion, chopped
- 3 tablespoons olive oil, divided
- ½ cup all-purpose flour
- 2 teaspoons salt
- 1 teaspoon black pepper
- 3 pounds boneless lamb for stew, cut into 2- to 2½-inch pieces
- 2 tablespoons sugar, divided
- 5 cups Slow Cooker Beef Stock
- 3 tablespoons tomato paste
- 4 cloves garlic, chopped
- 1 tablespoon dried thyme
- 1 tablespoon chopped fresh rosemary leaves
- 2 bay leaves
- 1 pound carrots, cut into 2-inch chunks
- 1 pound petite Yukon Gold potatoes, peeled and cut in half
- 1 package (10 ounces) frozen peas, thawed

1. Cook and stir onion in 1½ teaspoons oil in large skillet over medium heat until golden. Add to 6- to 7-quart **CROCK-POT®** slow cooker.

2. Combine flour, salt and pepper in large bowl. Dredge lamb in flour mixture. Heat 1 tablespoon oil in skillet over medium-high heat until hot. Add half of lamb; cook until browned on all sides. Add 1 tablespoon sugar; mix well to coat meat. Cook several minutes until meat is caramelized. Add meat to **CROCK-POT®** slow cooker. Repeat with remaining lamb, using remaining oil as needed and remaining tablespoon sugar.

3. Add stock to skillet. Bring to a boil over high heat, scraping sides and bottom of pan to loosen browned bits. Add tomato paste, garlic, thyme, rosemary and bay leaves. Mix well. Pour over meat mixture. Cover; cook on HIGH 2 hours or on LOW 4 hours.

4. Add carrots and potatoes. Cover; cook 1½ to 2½ hours on HIGH or 3 to 4 hours on LOW or until vegetables and lamb are tender.

5. Add peas. Cook 30 minutes more. Remove and discard bay leaves before serving.

Makes 6 to 8 servings

Beef, Lentil and Onion Soup

1. Spray large skillet with cooking spray. Heat skillet over medium-high heat until hot. Add beef; cook until browned on all sides.

2. Place carrots, celery and lentils in 3½- to 4-quart **CROCK-POT**® slow cooker. Top with beef. Sprinkle with thyme, pepper and salt. Pour water and soup over mixture. Cover; cook on HIGH 3½ to 4 hours or on LOW 7 to 8 hours or until meat and lentils are tender.

Makes 4 servings

Nonstick cooking spray
¾ pound lean boneless beef stew meat, cut into 1-inch pieces
2 cups chopped carrots
1 cup sliced celery
1 cup uncooked lentils
2 teaspoons dried thyme
¼ teaspoon black pepper
⅛ teaspoon salt
3¼ cups water
1 can (10½ ounces) condensed French onion soup, undiluted

beef and lamb

Curried Lamb and Swiss Chard Soup

2 tablespoons extra-virgin olive oil
1 small red onion, chopped
2 cloves garlic, minced
8 cups water
2 cups Swiss chard, trimmed, cleaned and chopped
2 cups green cabbage, cored, cleaned and chopped
2 cups dried cannellini beans, sorted and rinsed
2 lamb shanks
1 teaspoon salt
1 teaspoon curry powder
1 teaspoon black pepper
¼ cup lemon juice
1 teaspoon grated lemon peel
Fresh parsley (optional)

1. Heat oil in skillet over medium heat until hot. Add onion and garlic. Cook and stir 3 to 4 minutes or until tender. Transfer to 6- to 7-quart **CROCK-POT®** slow cooker.

2. Add water, Swiss chard, cabbage, beans, lamb shanks, salt, curry powder and pepper. Stir well to combine. Cover; cook on LOW 8 to 10 hours.

3. Transfer lamb shanks to cutting board and remove meat from bones. Dice meat and return to **CROCK-POT®** slow cooker. Add lemon juice. Stir well to combine. Garnish soup with lemon peel and parsley, if desired.

Makes 6 to 8 servings

Sweet and Sour Cabbage Soup

1. Cut chuck roast into 4 pieces. Spray 12-inch skillet with cooking spray. Heat over medium-high heat until hot. Brown meat on both sides. Place in 6- to 7-quart **CROCK-POT®** slow cooker. Add remaining ingredients in order listed. Cover; cook on LOW 6 to 8 hours.

2. Remove beef from **CROCK-POT®** slow cooker. Shred beef and return to soup; mix well.

- 2 pounds boneless chuck roast
- Nonstick cooking spray
- 1 can (about 28 ounces) diced tomatoes, undrained
- 1 can (15 ounces) tomato sauce
- 1 large onion, thinly sliced
- 3 carrots, shredded
- 2 pounds green cabbage, shredded
- 4 cups water
- ¾ cup sugar
- ½ cup lemon juice
- 1 tablespoon caraway seeds
- 2 teaspoons salt
- 1 teaspoon black pepper

Makes 8 to 10 servings

Veggie Soup with Beef

Place all ingredients in 4½-quart **CROCK-POT®** slow cooker. Add enough water to fill to within ½ inch of top. Cover; cook on LOW 8 to 10 hours.

- 1 pound beef stew meat
- 2 cans (15 ounces each) mixed vegetables
- 1 can (8 ounces) tomato sauce
- 2 cloves garlic, minced
- Water

Makes 4 servings

chicken and turkey

Chicken Miso Soup with Shiitake Mushrooms

1. Preheat oven to 500°F with rack in middle.

2. Pat chicken dry, then roast, skin side up, in 1 layer on 17×12-inch rimmed sheet pan or jelly-roll pan with sides until skin is golden brown, 35 to 40 minutes.

3. Transfer roasted chicken and pan liquids to bowl and spoon off fat that rises to surface. Add enough stock to bring liquid to 4 cups total.

4. Heat oil in skillet over medium heat and sauté onions until softened and beginning to brown. Add mushrooms, ginger and garlic, and sauté until garlic is golden, 3 to 5 minutes.

5. Add mirin to pan and bring to a boil, stirring and scraping up any brown bits for 1 minute. Pour into 6- to 7-quart **CROCK-POT**® slow cooker. Stir in miso paste and soy sauce, then add chicken, stock mixture and water. Cover and cook on HIGH 4 to 5 hours or on LOW 8 to 9 hours or until chicken is tender.

6. Stir in mustard greens and continue to cook, covered, 5 minutes or until greens are wilted. Taste and adjust seasonings as desired. Serve in shallow bowls with cooked white rice, if desired, and garnish with green onions.

- 16 chicken thighs (about 5 pounds) with skin and bone
- 3 to 4 cups Slow Cooker Chicken Stock
- 3 tablespoons canola oil
- 2 large onions, coarsely chopped
- 1 pound fresh shiitake mushrooms, stems discarded, large caps quartered
- 3 tablespoons finely chopped peeled ginger
- 3 tablespoons finely chopped garlic
- 1 cup mirin (Japanese sweet rice wine)
- 1 cup white miso paste
- ½ cup soy sauce
- 4 cups water
- 1 pound (about 16 cups) mustard greens, tough stems and ribs discarded and leaves coarsely chopped
- Cooked white rice (optional)
- Thinly sliced green onions, for garnish

Makes 6 to 8 servings

chicken and turkey

Vietnamese Chicken Pho

- 8 cups Slow Cooker Chicken Stock
- 2 to 3 cups cooked chicken, shredded
- 8 ounces bean sprouts
- Rice stick noodles
- 1 bunch Thai basil, chopped
- Hoisin sauce, for serving
- Lime wedges, for serving

1. Add stock and chicken to 3½- to 6-quart **CROCK-POT®** slow cooker. Cook on HIGH 3 hours or on LOW 6 to 7 hours.

2. Add bean sprouts, noodles and Thai basil. Heat until noodles are softened.

3. Spoon soup into individual serving bowls and serve with hoisin sauce and lime wedges.

Note: *A simple soup to prepare with leftover shredded chicken, this classic Asian chicken noodle soup packs tons of flavor.*

Makes 4 to 6 servings

chicken and turkey

Matzo Ball Soup

- 3 quarts (12 cups) Slow Cooker Chicken Stock
- 4 parsnips, peeled and sliced into ½-inch rounds
- 2 carrots, peeled and sliced into ½-inch rounds
- 3 leeks, sliced
- 1 large onion, sliced
- 1 small rotisserie chicken, cooked (optional)
- 1 tablespoon fresh dill
- Matzo Balls (recipe follows)
- Kosher salt and black pepper

1. Add stock to 6- to 7-quart **CROCK-POT®** slow cooker. Add parsnips, carrots, leeks and onion to stock and cook on HIGH 4 to 5 hours or on LOW 8 to 10 hours.

2. Remove skin and bones from chicken and cut into bite-sized pieces. Add chicken, if desired, dill and Matzo Balls to hot stock and cook on HIGH until heated through. Season to taste with salt and pepper and serve.

Makes 4 to 6 servings

Matzo Balls

- 4 large eggs
- 5 tablespoons butter or margarine, melted
- 1 small bunch flat-leaf parsley, minced
- 1 tablespoon fresh sage, minced
- 1¼ cups matzo meal
- ½ cup water
- Kosher salt and black pepper

1. Combine all ingredients in mixing bowl and blend with fork, making sure to generously season mixture with salt and pepper. Roll into golf ball-size or smaller matzo balls.

2. Cover and place in refrigerator 30 to 60 minutes.

3. Bring a pot of salted water to boil over medium-high heat. Drop matzo balls in and simmer for 20 minutes. Remove with a slotted spoon and reserve until needed.

chicken and turkey

Curried Chicken and Coconut Soup

- 6 cups Slow Cooker Chicken Stock
- 2 cans (13½ ounces each) unsweetened coconut milk
- 2 bunches green onions, sliced
- 3 to 4 tablespoons curry powder
- 4 stalks lemongrass, minced
- 2 tablespoons peeled and minced fresh ginger
- 8 large chicken thighs with bones, skin removed
- 2 packages (6 ounces each) baby spinach leaves
- 3 large limes, divided
- Salt and black pepper, to taste
- 1 bunch chopped fresh cilantro

1. Combine stock, coconut milk, green onions, curry powder, lemongrass, ginger and chicken in 3½- to 6-quart **CROCK-POT®** slow cooker. Cook on HIGH 6 hours or on LOW 10 hours.

2. Remove chicken from **CROCK-POT®** slow cooker to cutting board; let rest for a few minutes.

3. Remove bones and cut chicken into ½-inch cubes. Return chicken to soup; add spinach. Cook on HIGH until spinach wilts, about 10 minutes. Juice 2 limes and add juice to **CROCK-POT®** slow cooker. Season soup to taste with salt and pepper. Cut remaining lime into 6 to 8 wedges. Ladle soup into individual serving bowls; sprinkle with cilantro and serve with lime wedges.

Makes 6 to 8 servings

chicken and turkey

Chicken Tortilla Soup

- 4 boneless, skinless chicken thighs
- 2 cans (15 ounces each) diced tomatoes, undrained
- 1 can (4 ounces) chopped mild green chiles, drained
- ½ to 1 cup Slow Cooker Chicken Stock
- 1 yellow onion, diced
- 2 cloves garlic, minced
- 1 teaspoon ground cumin
- Salt and black pepper, to taste
- 4 corn tortillas, sliced into ¼-inch strips
- 2 tablespoons chopped fresh cilantro
- ½ cup shredded Monterey Jack cheese
- 1 avocado, peeled, diced and tossed with lime juice to prevent browning
- Lime wedges

1. Place chicken in 3½- to 5-quart **CROCK-POT®** slow cooker. Combine tomatoes with juice, chiles, ½ cup stock, onion, garlic and cumin in small bowl. Pour mixture over chicken.

2. Cover; cook on HIGH 3 hours or LOW 6 hours or until chicken is tender. Remove chicken from **CROCK-POT®** slow cooker. Shred with 2 forks. Return to cooking liquid. Adjust seasonings, adding salt, pepper and more stock as necessary.

3. Just before serving, add tortillas and cilantro to **CROCK-POT®** slow cooker. Stir to blend. Serve in soup bowls, topping each serving with cheese, avocado and a squeeze of lime juice.

Makes 4 to 6 servings

chicken and turkey

Cannellini Minestrone Soup

- 4 cups Slow Cooker Chicken Stock
- 1 can (14½ ounces) diced tomatoes, undrained
- 1 can (12 ounces) tomato-vegetable juice
- 2 cups escarole, cut into ribbons
- 1 cup chopped green onions
- 1 cup chopped carrots
- 1 cup chopped celery
- 1 cup chopped potatoes
- ¼ cup dried cannellini beans, sorted and rinsed
- 2 tablespoons chopped fresh chives
- 1 tablespoon chopped fresh flat-leaf parsley
- ¼ teaspoon salt
- ¼ teaspoon black pepper
- 2 ounces uncooked ditalini pasta

1. Place all ingredients except pasta in 5-quart **CROCK-POT®** slow cooker. Stir well to combine. Cover; cook on HIGH 4 to 6 hours or on LOW 6 to 8 hours.

2. Add pasta and stir. Cover; cook 20 minutes on HIGH or until pasta is al dente.

Makes 6 servings

chicken and turkey

Mediterranean Tomato, Oregano and Orzo Soup

- 2 tablespoons extra-virgin olive oil
- 1 large yellow onion, cut into wedges
- 3½ cups peeled* and hand-crushed fresh tomatoes or 1 can (28 ounces) peeled plum tomatoes
- 2 cups peeled and large-diced butternut squash
- 1 cup peeled and julienned carrots
- ½ cup sliced zucchini
- 1 tablespoon minced fresh bay leaves or 3 whole dried bay leaves
- 1 tablespoon chopped fresh oregano
- 1 can (15 ounces) garbanzo beans, drained and rinsed
- 2 cups Slow Cooker Chicken Stock
- 1 clove garlic, minced
- 1 teaspoon ground cumin
- ¾ teaspoon ground allspice
- ½ teaspoon salt
- ¼ teaspoon black pepper
- 1½ cups dried orzo pasta

*To peel tomatoes, place one at a time in simmering water about 10 seconds. (Add 30 seconds if tomatoes are not fully ripened.) Immediately plunge into bowl of cold water for 10 seconds. Peel skin with a knife.

1. Heat oil in skillet over medium heat until hot. Add onion. Cook and stir until translucent and soft, about 10 minutes.

2. Add tomatoes, squash, carrots, zucchini, bay leaves and oregano to skillet. Cook and stir 25 to 30 minutes longer. Transfer to 4½- to 6-quart **CROCK-POT**® slow cooker.

3. Add remaining ingredients, except orzo pasta. Cover; cook on HIGH 4 to 5 hours or on LOW 7 to 8 hours.

4. Turn **CROCK-POT**® slow cooker to HIGH. Add orzo. Cover; cook 30 to 45 minutes or until pasta is done. (Remove dried bay leaves before serving, if used.)

Makes 6 servings

chicken and turkey

Chicken and Chile Pepper Stew

- 1 pound boneless, skinless chicken thighs, cut into ½-inch pieces
- 1 pound small potatoes, cut lengthwise into halves, then crosswise into slices
- 1 cup chopped onion
- 2 poblano chile peppers, seeded and cut into ½-inch pieces*
- 1 jalapeño pepper, seeded and finely chopped*
- 3 cloves garlic, minced
- 3 cups Slow Cooker Chicken Stock
- 1 can (about 14 ounces) no-salt-added diced tomatoes, undrained
- 2 tablespoons chili powder
- 1 teaspoon dried oregano

*Poblano and jalapeño peppers can sting and irritate the skin, so wear rubber gloves when handling peppers and do not touch your eyes.

1. Place chicken, potatoes, onion, poblano peppers, jalapeño pepper and garlic in 4½- to 6-quart **CROCK-POT®** slow cooker.

2. Stir together stock, tomatoes, chili powder and oregano in large bowl. Pour stock mixture over chicken mixture in **CROCK-POT®** slow cooker; mix well. Cover; cook on LOW 8 to 9 hours.

Makes 6 servings

chicken and turkey

Curried Butternut Squash Soup

- 2 pounds butternut squash, peeled, seeded and chopped into 1-inch cubes
- 1 firm crisp apple, peeled, seeded and chopped
- 1 yellow onion, chopped
- 5 cups Slow Cooker Chicken Stock
- 1 tablespoon curry powder, sweet or hot
- ¼ teaspoon ground cloves
- Salt and black pepper, to taste
- ¼ cup chopped dried cranberries (optional)

1. Place squash, apple and onion in 4½- to 6-quart **CROCK-POT®** slow cooker.

2. Mix together stock, curry powder and cloves in small bowl. Pour mixture into **CROCK-POT®** slow cooker. Cover; cook on HIGH 4 hours or on LOW 5 to 5½ hours or until vegetables are tender.

3. Process in blender, in 2 or 3 batches, to desired consistency. Add salt and pepper. Garnish with cranberries, if desired.

Makes 6 to 8 servings

Roasted Corn and Red Pepper Chowder

1. Heat oil in skillet over medium heat until hot. Add corn, bell pepper and onions. Cook and stir until vegetables are tender and lightly browned, about 7 to 8 minutes. Transfer to 3½- to 4½-quart **CROCK-POT®** slow cooker.

2. Add stock, potatoes, salt and pepper. Stir well to combine. Cover; cook on HIGH 4 to 5 hours or on LOW 7 to 9 hours.

3. Add milk 30 minutes before serving. Stir well to combine. To serve, garnish with parsley.

Makes 4 servings

- 2 tablespoons extra-virgin olive oil
- 2 cups fresh corn kernels or frozen corn, thawed
- 1 red bell pepper, cored, seeded and diced
- 2 green onions, sliced
- 4 cups Slow Cooker Chicken Stock
- 2 baking potatoes, peeled and diced
- 1 teaspoon salt
- ½ teaspoon black pepper
- 1 can (13 ounces) evaporated milk
- 2 tablespoons minced flat-leaf parsley

chicken and turkey

Southwestern Turkey Tenderloin Stew

1½ pounds turkey tenderloins, cut into ¾-inch pieces
1 tablespoon chili powder
1 teaspoon ground cumin
¼ teaspoon salt
1 can (15 ounces) chili beans in spicy sauce, undrained
1 can (14½ ounces) chili-style stewed tomatoes, undrained
¾ cup salsa or picante sauce
1 red bell pepper, seeded and cut into ¾-inch pieces
1 green bell pepper, seeded and cut into ¾-inch pieces
¾ cup chopped red or yellow onion
3 cloves garlic, minced
Fresh cilantro (optional)

1. Place turkey in 4½- to 5-quart **CROCK-POT®** slow cooker. Sprinkle with chili powder, cumin and salt; toss to coat.

2. Add beans, tomatoes with juice, salsa, bell peppers, onion and garlic; mix well. Cover; cook on LOW 5 to 6 hours.

3. Adjust seasonings. Ladle into bowls. Garnish with cilantro, if desired.

Makes 6 servings

Thai-Style Chicken and Pumpkin Soup

1. Heat oil in large nonstick skillet over medium heat. Add chicken and cook, stirring occasionally, about 3 minutes. Add onion, garlic, ginger and red pepper flakes; cook 1 or 2 minutes longer or until mixture is fragrant.

2. Transfer chicken mixture to 4½- to 5-quart **CROCK-POT®** slow cooker. Add celery, carrots, pumpkin, mango nectar, lime juice, peanut butter, stock and water; stir to combine. Cover; cook on HIGH 4 hours or on LOW 8 hours.

3. Stir in rice vinegar and ¼ cup cilantro. Mix cream and cornstarch together in small mixing bowl. Stir mixture into soup. Turn setting to HIGH. Simmer, uncovered, 10 minutes or until soup thickens.

4. To serve, put rice in soup bowls. Ladle soup around rice. Sprinkle with remaining cilantro, green onions and peanuts. Squeeze fresh lime juice over soup, if desired.

Makes 4 to 6 servings

- 1 tablespoon extra-virgin olive oil
- 6 boneless, skinless chicken breasts, cut into 1-inch cubes
- 1 large white onion, thinly sliced
- 3 cloves garlic, minced
- 1 tablespoon minced fresh ginger
- ½ to ¾ teaspoon crushed red pepper flakes
- 2 stalks celery, trimmed and diced
- 2 carrots, peeled, trimmed and diced
- 1 can (15 ounces) solid-pack pumpkin
- ½ cup mango nectar
- ½ cup fresh lime juice
- ½ cup creamy peanut butter
- 4 cups Slow Cooker Chicken Stock
- 2 cups water
- 3 tablespoons rice vinegar
- ½ cup minced fresh cilantro, divided
- ½ cup heavy cream
- 1 tablespoon cornstarch
- 2 to 4 cups hot cooked rice (preferably jasmine or basmati)
- 3 green onions, minced
- ½ cup roasted unsalted peanuts, coarsely chopped
- Lime wedges (optional)

• pork, ham and sausage

Northwoods Smoked Ham and Bean Soup

1. Heat olive oil in skillet over medium heat. Add onions and cook, stirring occasionally, until soft and fragrant, about 10 minutes. Add garlic and cook 1 minute.

2. Place onion and garlic mixture, stock, ham hocks, ham, tomatoes, parsley, thyme and bay leaves in 5- to 7-quart **CROCK-POT®** slow cooker. Cook on HIGH 6 hours or on LOW 10 hours.

3. Stir in beans and pasta and continue to cook on HIGH until heated through.

4. Season to taste with salt and pepper and serve.

Makes 6 to 8 servings

- 2 tablespoons olive oil
- 2 large onions, chopped
- 6 cloves garlic, peeled and minced
- 6 cups Slow Cooker Chicken Stock
- 2 smoked ham hocks
- 2 cups cubed cooked smoked ham
- 1 can (28 ounces) whole peeled plum tomatoes, drained and coarsely chopped
- 1 bunch fresh parsley, stemmed and chopped
- 4 sprigs fresh thyme
- 4 bay leaves
- 2 cans (15 ounces each) cannellini beans, drained and rinsed
- ½ pound cooked orchiette, cavatelli or ditalini pasta
- Kosher salt and black pepper

pork, ham and sausage

Soupe au Pistou

- 2 tablespoons olive oil
- ¼ pound pancetta, chopped
- 2 onions, chopped
- 2 cloves garlic, mashed
- 2 leeks, diced
- ½ pound small zucchini, diced
- 1 can (15 ounces) lima beans, rinsed and drained
- 1 can (14 ounces) diced plum tomatoes or 3 to 4 fresh plum tomatoes, chopped
- 6 to 8 cups Slow Cooker Chicken Stock
- ½ pound fresh green beans, cut into 1½-inch pieces
- 2 cans (15 ounces each) cannellini beans, drained and rinsed
- ½ pound small pasta, such as ditalini, cooked al dente
- Salt and black pepper
- ½ cup Parmesan cheese, grated
- 6 tablespoons butter
- 3 cloves garlic, minced
- 2 bunches fresh basil leaves, chopped

1. Heat oil in skillet over medium heat. Add pancetta, onions, garlic and leeks and cook, stirring, until softened. Transfer mixture to 6- to 7-quart **CROCK-POT®** slow cooker.

2. Add zucchini, lima beans, tomatoes and enough stock to cover vegetables. Cover and cook on HIGH 3½ hours or on LOW 6 to 7 hours.

3. Add green beans, cannellini beans and pasta. Cover and cook an additional 15 minutes on HIGH or until green beans are crisp-tender and bright green. Season to taste with salt and pepper.

4. For garnish, combine Parmesan, butter, garlic, and basil in food processor. Use on/off pulses to make coarse paste. Ladle soup into individual bowls and garnish with Parmesan mixture. Serve with crusty French bread.

Makes 6 to 8 servings

pork, ham and sausage

Roast Pork Soup with Soba Noodles and Bok Choy

- 2 tablespoons hoisin sauce
- 1 tablespoon sugar
- 1 to 2 teaspoons Chinese 5-spice powder
- 1 (2½-pound) pork loin
- 6 cups Slow Cooker Chicken Stock
- 1½ tablespoons fresh ginger, peeled and cut into thin slices
- 3 cloves garlic, thinly sliced
- 2 tablespoons soy sauce
- 1 head bok choy, sliced
- 1 pound soba noodles, cooked

1. Preheat oven to 350°F. In small bowl, combine hoisin sauce, sugar and five spice powder. Baste pork with sauce and roast 45 to 60 minutes, or until just cooked through.

2. Let meat rest 15 minutes and slice into thin matchstick pieces.

3. Place pork in 5- to 7-quart **CROCK-POT®** slow cooker and add stock, ginger, garlic, soy sauce and bok choy. Cook on HIGH 3 to 4 hours or on LOW 6 to 7 hours.

4. Stir in soba noodles and cook until just heated through.

Makes 6 to 8 servings

pork, ham and sausage

Nana's Mini Meatball Soup

1 pound ground beef
1 pound ground pork
1½ cups finely grated Pecorino Romano or Parmesan cheese
1 cup Italian bread crumbs
2 eggs
1 bunch flat-leaf parsley
Kosher salt and black pepper
3 quarts Slow Cooker Chicken Stock
1 bunch escarole, coarsely chopped
½ box (8 ounces) ditalini pasta, cooked

1. Combine beef, pork, cheese, bread crumbs, eggs, parsley, salt and pepper in large bowl. Mix well by hand and roll into ¾-inch meatballs.

2. Add meatballs and chicken stock to 6- to 7-quart **CROCK-POT®** slow cooker. Cook on HIGH 5 hours or on LOW 9 hours.

3. Add escarole and cook until escarole has wilted and is bright green and tender, about 15 minutes. Add cooked ditalini to soup and serve.

Tip: Substitute spinach for escarole, if desired.

Makes 6 to 8 servings

pork, ham and sausage

Country Sausage and Bean Stew

- 3 to 4 cups Slow Cooker Chicken Stock
- 1½ cups hot water
- 1 cup dried black beans, rinsed and sorted
- 1 cup chopped yellow onion
- 2 bay leaves
- 1 teaspoon sugar substitute
- ⅛ teaspoon ground red pepper
- Nonstick cooking spray
- 6 ounces reduced-fat country pork sausage
- 1 cup chopped tomato
- 1 tablespoon chili powder
- 1 tablespoon Worcestershire sauce
- 2 teaspoons olive oil
- 1½ teaspoons ground cumin
- ½ teaspoon salt
- ¼ cup chopped fresh cilantro

1. Combine stock, water, beans, onion, bay leaves, sugar substitute and red pepper in 3½- to 4-quart **CROCK-POT®** slow cooker. Cover; cook on HIGH 4 hours or on LOW 8 hours.

2. Coat 10-inch nonstick skillet with cooking spray. Heat over medium-high heat until hot. Add sausage; cook until beginning to brown, stirring to break up large pieces. Drain fat.

3. Add sausage to bean mixture in **CROCK-POT®** slow cooker, along with remaining ingredients except cilantro. Cover; cook on HIGH 15 minutes. Top with cilantro before serving.

Makes 9 servings

pork, ham and sausage

Sausage, Butter Bean and Cabbage Soup

- 2 tablespoons butter, divided
- 1 large onion, chopped
- 12 ounces smoked sausage such as kielbasa or andouille, cut into ½-inch slices
- 8 cups Slow Cooker Chicken Stock
- ½ head savoy cabbage, coarsely shredded
- 3 tablespoons tomato paste
- 1 bay leaf
- 4 medium tomatoes, chopped
- 2 cans (14 ounces each) butter beans, drained
- Salt and black pepper

Handwritten: Sliced Potatoes, Baby Carrots, onions baby

1. Melt 1 tablespoon butter in large skillet over medium heat. Add onion; cook and stir 3 to 4 minutes or until golden. Place in 3½- to 4½-quart **CROCK-POT®** slow cooker.

2. Melt remaining 1 tablespoon butter in same skillet; cook sausage until brown. Add to **CROCK-POT®** slow cooker.

3. Place stock, cabbage, tomato paste and bay leaf in **CROCK-POT®** slow cooker; stir until well blended. Cover; cook on LOW 4 hours or HIGH 2 hours.

4. Add tomatoes and beans; season with salt and pepper. Cover; cook 1 hour on HIGH or until heated through. Remove and discard bay leaf.

Tip: Savoy cabbage is an excellent cooking cabbage with a full head of crinkled leaves varying from dark to pale green. Green cabbage may be substituted.

Makes 6 servings

pork, ham and sausage

Gumbo

- ¼ pound bacon, cooked and chopped
- 2 large onions, chopped
- 2 pounds boneless, skinless chicken thighs
- 4 stalks celery, chopped
- 1 green bell pepper, seeded and diced
- 1 red bell pepper, seeded and diced
- 2 jalapeños, seeded and diced*
- 8 cups Slow Cooker Chicken Stock
- 1 can (28 ounces) whole peeled plum tomatoes, undrained
- 2 cups fresh okra, ends trimmed and sliced in ¼-inch pieces
- 1 cup converted rice
- 2 tablespoons fresh parsley, minced
- Kosher salt and black pepper
- Filé powder (ground sassafras leaves) for serving

*Jalapeño peppers can sting and irritate the skin, so wear rubber gloves when handling peppers and do not touch your eyes.

1. Place bacon, onions, chicken, celery, bell peppers, jalapeños and stock in 6- to 7-quart **CROCK-POT**® slow cooker. Cover and cook on LOW 5 to 6 hours or on HIGH 3 hours.

2. Remove cooked chicken and cut into 1-inch pieces. Add tomatoes and their juice, okra, rice, parsley, salt and pepper. Cook on HIGH 1 hour.

3. Taste and adjust seasonings. Ladle into individual bowls and serve. Keep filé powder on table for use as desired.

Tip: This dish can be spiced up with hot sauce, and shrimp or crawfish can be added for even more Louisiana flavor.

Makes 6 to 8 servings

Split Pea Soup with Andouille Sausage

1. Brown sausage in heavy skillet over medium heat. Using a slotted spoon, transfer to paper towels to drain, and pour off all but 1 tablespoon fat from skillet.

2. Add onion, celery and garlic to skillet and cook over medium heat, stirring frequently, until celery is softened. Place sausage, onion, celery and garlic in 5- to 7-quart **CROCK-POT®** slow cooker. Add split peas, stock, water, thyme, bay leaf and carrots. Cover and cook on HIGH 4 to 5 hours or on LOW 7 to 9 hours, or until carrots are tender.

3. Discard bay leaf, season soup with salt and pepper and serve with croutons or bread.

Tip: *Drizzle finished soup with an aged balsamic vinegar or top with shredded sharp Cheddar cheese, if desired.*

- 1½ pounds smoked andouille sausage, sliced thin
- 1 onion, chopped
- 1 stalk celery, finely chopped
- 2 cloves garlic, minced
- 1 pound split peas, picked over
- 4 cups Slow Cooker Chicken Stock
- 4 cups water
- ½ teaspoon dried thyme
- 1 bay leaf
- 2 carrots, peeled and diced
- Salt and black pepper
- Croutons or crusty bread

Makes 6 to 8 servings

pork, ham and sausage

Lentil Soup with Ham and Bacon

- 8 ounces chopped bacon
- 8 cups Slow Cooker Beef Stock
- 1½ pounds dried lentils
- 2 cups chopped ham
- 1 cup chopped carrots
- ¾ cup chopped celery
- ¾ cup chopped tomatoes
- ½ cup chopped onions
- 2 teaspoons salt
- 2 teaspoons black pepper
- ½ teaspoon dried marjoram

1. Heat skillet over medium heat until hot. Add bacon. Cook and stir until crisp. Transfer to 4½- to 6-quart **CROCK-POT®** slow cooker using slotted spoon.

2. Add remaining ingredients. Cover; cook on HIGH 6 to 8 hours or on LOW 8 to 10 hours, or until lentils are tender.

Makes 8 servings

Panama Pork Stew

- 2 small sweet potatoes (about ¾ pound), peeled and cut into 2-inch pieces
- 1 package (10 ounces) frozen corn
- 1 package (9 ounces) frozen cut green beans
- 1 cup chopped onion
- 1¼ pounds pork stew meat, cut into 1-inch cubes
- 1 can (14½ ounces) diced tomatoes
- ¼ cup water
- 1 to 2 tablespoons chili powder
- ½ teaspoon salt
- ½ teaspoon ground coriander

1. Place potatoes, corn, green beans and onion in 4½-quart **CROCK-POT®** slow cooker. Top with pork.

2. Combine tomatoes, water, chili powder, salt and coriander in medium bowl. Pour mixture over pork in **CROCK-POT®** slow cooker.

3. Cover; cook on LOW 7 to 9 hours.

Makes 6 servings

Black Bean Soup

1. Combine all ingredients in 3½- to 6-quart **CROCK-POT®** slow cooker and stir well. Cover and cook on HIGH 4 to 5 hours or on LOW 8 to 10 hours.

2. Taste, adjust seasoning with salt and pepper to taste, and serve with desired garnishes.

Makes 4 to 6 servings

- 3 cans (15 ounces each) black beans, rinsed and drained
- 3½ cups Slow Cooker Beef Stock
- 4 plum tomatoes, diced
- 2 jalapeños, minced*
- ½ pound bacon, cooked and crumbled
- 1 large onion, chopped
- ⅓ cup red wine vinegar
- 1 teaspoon dried oregano leaves
- 1½ teaspoons ground cumin
- 1 teaspoon dried thyme leaves
- Kosher salt and black pepper, to taste
- Diced avocado, lime juice and Cheddar cheese, for garnish (optional)

*Jalapeño peppers can sting and irritate the skin, so wear rubber gloves when handling peppers and do not touch your eyes.

seafood

Zuppa de Clams

1. Heat oil in skillet over medium heat. Add onion, mushrooms and chorizo, and cook, stirring, until onion is softened, about 8 minutes. Transfer to 4- to 7-quart **CROCK-POT®** slow cooker.

2. Add vermouth, tomato sauce and wine. Cover and cook on HIGH 3½ hours or on LOW 6 to 7 hours. Add clams and cook 10 to 15 minutes more, or until clams open. Discard any clams that do not open and serve.

Serving suggestion: *Serve with crusty Italian bread or over cooked pasta.*

- 4 tablespoons extra-virgin olive oil
- 1 red onion, peeled and diced
- 1 package (8 ounces) shiitake mushrooms
- ½ pound cooked chorizo sausage, thinly sliced
- ½ cup sweet red vermouth
- 1½ cups homemade or best quality tomato sauce
- 1 cup dry white wine
- 24 littleneck clams, scrubbed and rinsed

seafood

Thai Shrimp Soup Infused with Lemongrass, Ginger and Chiles

- ¾ pound large shrimp, peeled and deveined, shells reserved
- 8 cups Slow Cooker Fish Stock or Slow Cooker Chicken Stock
- 1 cup diced carrots
- 3 stalks lemongrass, thinly sliced
- 2 to 3 tablespoons fresh ginger, peeled and grated
- 2 tablespoons minced garlic
- 1½ tablespoons finely chopped fresh Thai basil or basil
- 1½ tablespoons finely chopped fresh mint
- 1½ tablespoons finely chopped cilantro
- 1 serrano chile, stemmed, thinly sliced
- 1 to 2 limes, juiced
- 1 can unsweetened coconut milk
- ¼ to ½ teaspoon sambal oelek chile paste*
- 6 thin lime slices

*Chile pepper pastes, such as sambal oelek, are commonly used condiments in Southeast Asia. You can find them in the ethnic section of many grocery stores, in Asian markets or online.

1. Halve shrimp lengthwise. Place in refrigerator.

2. Place shrimp shells, stock, carrots, lemongrass, ginger and garlic in 3½- to 7-quart **CROCK-POT®** slow cooker. Cook on HIGH 2 to 3 hours or LOW 3½ to 4½ hours.

3. Strain broth and return to **CROCK-POT®** slow cooker; discard solids. Add shrimp, Thai basil, mint, cilantro, chile, lime juice, coconut milk and chile paste. Cover and cook on HIGH until shrimp are cooked through, about 15 minutes.

4. Taste and adjust seasonings. Ladle soup into serving bowls and garnish with lime slices.

Makes 6 servings

seafood

Scallop and Corn Chowder

- 6 tablespoons butter, divided
- 1 bunch leeks, cleaned well and diced
- ¾ pound pancetta, diced
- 5 small Yukon Gold potatoes, diced
- 5¼ cups Slow Cooker Fish Stock
- 2 cups corn
- 1 to 2 tablespoons minced fresh thyme, divided
- 4 tablespoons all-purpose flour
- 1 pound sea scallops, quartered
- 1 pint heavy cream
- Freshly ground black pepper

1. Heat 2 tablespoons butter in skillet over medium-high heat. Add leeks and cook, stirring, until softened and just beginning to brown. Transfer to 5½- to 7-quart **CROCK-POT®** slow cooker.

2. In same skillet over medium heat, cook pancetta until lightly browned; transfer to **CROCK-POT®** slow cooker. Add potatoes, stock, corn and ½ to 1 tablespoon thyme. Cover and cook on HIGH 2 to 3 hours or LOW 4 to 6 hours, or until potatoes are tender.

3. In large saucepan, combine 4 tablespoons butter and flour and stir constantly 5 minutes over medium heat to make roux. Stir in 2 large ladles of stock from **CROCK-POT®** slow cooker. Stir until fully combined and return mixture to **CROCK-POT®** slow cooker, stirring until roux blends with stock. Add scallops and cook about 10 minutes or until scallops are just cooked through.

4. Stir in cream and garnish with pepper and remaining thyme.

Makes 6 to 8 servings

seafood

Seafood Bouillabaisse

½ bulb fennel, chopped
1 medium onion, chopped
2 cloves garlic, minced
2 bottles (12 ounces each) beer, divided
1 can (28 ounces) tomato purée
8 ounces clam juice
1 bay leaf
½ teaspoon salt
¼ teaspoon black pepper
2 cups water
½ pound red snapper, pin bones removed and cut into 1-inch pieces
8 mussels, scrubbed and debearded
8 cherry stone clams
8 large shrimp, shells on
4 lemon wedges
Flat-leaf parsley sprigs (optional)

1. Coat skillet with nonstick cooking spray and heat over medium-high heat. Add fennel, onion and garlic and cook, stirring, until onion is soft and translucent. Transfer vegetables to 5-quart **CROCK-POT®** slow cooker. Add 1 bottle beer, tomato purée, clam juice, bay leaf, salt and pepper. Cover and cook on HIGH 3 to 4 hours or on LOW 6 to 8 hours.

2. During last 30 minutes of cooking time, pour remaining bottle beer into large stockpot. Add 2 cups water. Place steamer insert in stockpot (do not allow water to touch the insert). Bring to boil. Place snapper, mussels, clams and shrimp into insert. Cover and steam 4 to 8 minutes, discarding any mussels or clams that do not open.

3. Remove bay leaf from tomato broth. Ladle broth into wide soup bowl. Place mussels, clams, shrimp and fish on top of broth. Squeeze lemon over fish and seafood, and garnish with parsley sprig, if desired.

Makes 4 servings

seafood

New England Clam Chowder

- 6 slices bacon, diced
- 2 onions, chopped
- 5 cans (6½ ounces each) clams, drained and liquid reserved
- 6 medium red potatoes, cubed
- 2 tablespoons minced garlic
- 1 teaspoon black pepper
- 2 cans (12 ounces each) evaporated milk
- Salt, to taste

1. Cook and stir bacon and onions in medium skillet until onions are tender. Place in 4½- to 6-quart **CROCK-POT®** slow cooker.

2. Add enough water to reserved clam liquid to make 3 cups. Pour into **CROCK-POT®** slow cooker, and add potatoes, garlic and pepper. Cover; cook on HIGH 1 to 3 hours or on LOW 5 to 8 hours.

3. Turn **CROCK-POT®** slow cooker to LOW and mix in clams and milk. Cover; cook 30 to 45 minutes. Adjust seasoning, if necessary.

Tip: *Shellfish and mollusks are delicate and should be added to the* **CROCK-POT®** *slow cooker during the last 15 to 30 minutes of the cooking time if you're using the HIGH heat setting, and during the last 30 to 45 minutes if you're using the LOW setting. This type of seafood overcooks easily, becoming tough and rubbery, so watch your cooking times, and cook only long enough for foods to be done.*

Makes 6 to 8 servings

seafood

Potato-Crab Chowder

- 1 package (10 ounces) frozen corn, thawed
- 1 cup frozen hash brown potatoes, thawed
- ¾ cup finely chopped carrots
- 1 teaspoon dried thyme leaves
- ¾ teaspoon garlic-pepper
- 3 cups Slow Cooker Chicken Stock
- ½ cup water
- 1 cup evaporated milk
- 3 tablespoons cornstarch
- 1 can (6 ounces) crabmeat, drained
- ½ cup sliced green onions

1. Place corn, potatoes and carrots in 4½-quart **CROCK-POT®** slow cooker. Sprinkle with thyme and garlic-pepper. Add stock and water.

2. Cover; cook on LOW 3½ to 4½ hours.

3. Blend evaporated milk and cornstarch until smooth. Stir into **CROCK-POT®** slow cooker. Cover; cook on HIGH 15 to 30 minutes. Just before serving, stir in crabmeat and green onions.

Makes 5 servings

seafood

Cod Fish Stew

½ pound bacon, coarsely chopped
1 large carrot, diced
1 large onion, diced
2 stalks celery, diced
2 cloves garlic, minced
 Kosher salt and black pepper
1 can (28 ounces) plum tomatoes, drained
3 tablespoons tomato paste
½ cup white wine
3 tablespoons chopped flat-leaf parsley
3 cups water
2 cups clam juice or fish stock
3 saffron threads
2 potatoes, peeled and diced
2½ pounds fresh cod, skinned and cut into bite-sized pieces

1. In skillet over medium-high heat, cook bacon until crisp. Remove with slotted spoon. Add carrot, onion, celery and garlic to skillet, season with salt and pepper and cook, stirring, until vegetables soften.

2. Place bacon and vegetables in 5½- to 7-quart **CROCK-POT®** slow cooker. Stir in tomatoes, tomato paste, wine, parsley, water, clam juice, saffron and potatoes. Cook on HIGH 3 to 4 hours or on LOW 6 to 7 hours, or until potatoes are tender.

3. Add cod and cook 10 to 20 minutes, or until cod is just cooked through.

Note: Cod is a great fish to use for soup or stew. The thick creamy white fish becomes a hearty meal when paired with bacon and tomato.

Makes 6 to 8 servings

Cioppino

1. Combine fish pieces, mushrooms, carrots, onion, green pepper, garlic, tomato sauce, stock, salt, black pepper and oregano in 4½-quart **CROCK-POT®** slow cooker. Cover; cook on LOW 10 to 12 hours.

2. Turn **CROCK-POT®** slow cooker to HIGH. Add clams, shrimp and crabmeat. Cover; cook 30 minutes or until seafood is heated through. Garnish with parsley before serving.

Makes 6 servings

- 1 pound cod, halibut or any firm-fleshed white fish, cubed
- 1 cup sliced mushrooms
- 2 carrots, sliced
- 1 onion, chopped
- 1 green pepper, chopped
- 1 teaspoon minced garlic
- 1 can (15 ounces) tomato sauce
- 1½ to 2 cups Slow Cooker Fish Stock or Slow Cooker Beef Stock
- 1 teaspoon salt
- ½ teaspoon black pepper
- ½ teaspoon dried oregano
- 1 can (7 ounces) cooked clams
- ½ pound cooked shrimp
- 1 package (6 ounces) cooked crabmeat
- Minced fresh parsley

seafood

Creamy Seafood Chowder

- 1 quart (4 cups) half-and-half
- 2 cans (14½ ounces each) whole white potatoes, drained and cubed
- 2 cans (10¾ ounces each) condensed cream of mushroom soup, undiluted
- 1 bag (16 ounces) frozen hash brown potatoes, thawed
- 1 medium onion, minced
- ½ cup (1 stick) butter, diced
- 1 teaspoon salt
- 1 teaspoon black pepper
- 5 cans (about 8 ounces each) whole oysters, drained and rinsed
- 2 cans (about 6 ounces each) minced clams
- 2 cans (about 4 ounces each) cocktail shrimp, drained and rinsed

1. Combine half-and-half, canned potatoes, soup, frozen potatoes, onion, butter, salt and pepper in 5- to 6-quart **CROCK-POT®** slow cooker. Mix well.

2. Cover; cook on LOW 3 to 4 hours.

3. Add oysters, clams and shrimp; stir gently. Cover; cook on LOW 30 to 45 minutes or until seafood is done.

Makes 8 to 10 servings

Creamy Crab Bisque

1. Combine cream, crab, butter, lemon peel, lemon juice, nutmeg and allspice in 4½- to 6-quart **CROCK-POT®** slow cooker. Stir well to combine. Cover; cook on LOW 1 to 2 hours.

2. Stir in wine. Add mandlen crumbs to thicken soup and stir again. Continue cooking 10 minutes longer.

Makes 6 to 8 servings

- 4 cups heavy cream
- 3 cups fresh crabmeat, flaked and picked over
- 3 tablespoons unsalted butter
- 2 teaspoons grated lemon peel
- 1 teaspoon lemon juice
- ½ teaspoon ground nutmeg
- ¼ teaspoon ground allspice
- 3 tablespoons dry red wine
- ½ cup prepared mandlen* (soup nuts), ground into crumbs

*Mandlen are small nugget-like crackers made from matzo meal, available in the supermarket ethnic foods aisle.

vegetable

Corn Chowder with Basil Oil

1. Melt butter in skillet over medium-high heat. Add leeks; cook and stir until softened and just beginning to brown.

2. Place leeks in 3- to 6-quart **CROCK-POT®** slow cooker and add stock, corn, thyme, salt and pepper. Cook on HIGH 4 to 6 hours or on LOW 8 to 10 hours.

3. Stir in cream and cook until just heated through.

4. Ladle into individual soup bowls and drizzle with Basil Oil as desired.

Makes 6 to 8 servings

- 3 tablespoons butter
- 3 leeks, cleaned well and sliced or 2 onions, peeled and diced
- 4 cups Slow Cooker Vegetable Stock
- 5 cups frozen corn
- 3 sprigs fresh thyme, stemmed
- Kosher salt and black pepper
- ½ cup heavy cream
- Basil Oil (recipe follows)

Basil Oil

1. Place basil and oil in blender and process until smooth. Place purée into saucepan over medium heat and bring to a simmer; simmer 30 seconds. Remove from heat.

2. Strain oil through a fine mesh sieve suspended over a bowl. Do not stir or push paste through sieve.

3. Discard solids and store Basil Oil in refrigerator up to 3 days.

- 3 cups fresh basil
- 1 cup olive oil

vegetable

Autumn Apple and Squash Soup

- 5 tablespoons butter
- 2½ pounds butternut squash, peeled, seeded and cut into ½-inch pieces (about 6 cups)
- 2 large red onions
- 3 to 4 large stalks celery
- 3 large green apples, peeled, cored and coarsely chopped
- 2 to 3 sprigs fresh thyme, stemmed
- 10 fresh sage leaves, minced
- 4 cups Slow Cooker Vegetable Stock
- Kosher salt and black pepper
- ½ cup pepitas*
- 1 tablespoon honey
- 1 tablespoon water
- Crumbled blue cheese, to garnish
- Extra-virgin olive oil, to garnish

*Pepitas, or shelled pumpkin seeds, are available at specialty and Latin food stores and make a great garnish to almost any soup or salad. They can be sweetened and spiced as desired and lightly toasted in a skillet on the stovetop.

1. Melt butter in large, heavy saucepan over medium-high heat. Add squash, onions and celery; cook and stir until slightly softened, about 15 minutes. Place vegetables in 5- to 7-quart **CROCK-POT®** slow cooker. Mix in apples, thyme and sage. Add stock and cook on HIGH 8 hours or on LOW 12 hours.

2. Working in batches, purée soup in blender, pulsing to achieve a coarser or smoother texture as desired. Return soup to stoneware. Set **CROCK-POT®** slow cooker to WARM. (If soup has cooled considerably, set to HIGH.) Taste and adjust seasonings.

3. Combine pepitas with honey and water in small skillet over medium heat. Toast lightly. Ladle soup into bowls. Top with honeyed pepitas and blue cheese, and drizzle with olive oil.

Variations: Add lump crabmeat or serve with cinnamon and butter toasted croutons.

Makes 6 to 8 servings

vegetable

Orange Soup

- 2 tablespoons olive oil
- 1 small onion, minced
- ¼ cup peeled, minced fresh ginger
- 4 to 5 cups peeled, sliced carrots (about 1½ pounds)
- 3 to 4 cups Slow Cooker Vegetable Stock, divided
- 1⅓ cups orange juice
- ½ cup half-and-half
- Salt and black pepper

1. Heat oil in large, heavy saucepan over medium-high heat. Add onion and ginger; cook and stir until onion is translucent, about 5 minutes.

2. Place onions and ginger in 3½- to 7-quart **CROCK-POT®** slow cooker, add carrots and 3 cups stock. Cover and cook on HIGH 3 to 4 hours or on LOW 7 to 8 hours.

3. Using an immersion blender, blender or food processor, purée soup then return to **CROCK-POT®** slow cooker. Stir in orange juice and half-and-half, and cook on HIGH 15 to 20 minutes or until heated through. Do not simmer. Season soup to taste with salt and pepper. Thin with remaining stock as desired.

Makes 6 to 8 servings

vegetable

Spring Pea and Mint Broth Soup

8 cups water

3 carrots, cut into chunks

2 onions, coarsely chopped

2 to 3 leeks, cleaned well and coarsely chopped

2 stalks celery, cut into chunks

1 bunch fresh mint

3 to 4 cups fresh spring peas or 1 bag (32 ounces) frozen peas

1 tablespoon fresh lemon juice

Kosher salt and black pepper

Crème fraîche or sour cream

1. Combine water, carrots, onions, leeks, celery and mint in 4½- to 6-quart **CROCK-POT**® slow cooker. Cook on HIGH 5 hours.

2. Strain broth and return to **CROCK-POT**® slow cooker. Discard solids. Add peas and lemon juice. Cook on HIGH 2 to 3 hours or on LOW 4 to 5 hours.

3. Season with salt and pepper. Ladle soup into bowls and garnish with dollop of crème fraîche.

Note: *Whether using farmstand-fresh spring peas or frozen sweet peas, this soup is fun to make. The aroma of fresh mint that fills the house is reason enough to try it.*

Makes 6 to 8 servings

vegetable

Lentil Stew over Couscous

- 1 large onion, chopped
- 1 green bell pepper, chopped
- 4 stalks celery, chopped
- 1 medium carrot, cut lengthwise in half, then cut into 1-inch pieces
- 2 cloves garlic, chopped
- 3 cups dried lentils (1 pound), sorted and rinsed
- 1 can (14½ ounces) diced tomatoes, undrained
- 1½ to 2 cups Slow Cooker Vegetable Stock or Slow Cooker Chicken Stock
- 3 cups water
- ¼ teaspoon black pepper
- 1 teaspoon dried marjoram leaves
- 1 tablespoon cider vinegar
- 1 tablespoon olive oil
- 4½ to 5 cups hot cooked couscous
- Carrot curls (optional)
- Celery leaves (optional)

1. Combine onion, bell pepper, celery, carrot, garlic, lentils, tomatoes with juice, stock, water, black pepper and marjoram in 6- to 7-quart **CROCK-POT®** slow cooker. Stir; cover and cook on LOW 8 to 9 hours or until vegetables are tender.

2. Stir in vinegar and olive oil. Serve over couscous. Garnish with carrot curls and celery leaves, if desired.

Tip: Lentil stew keeps well in the refrigerator for up to 1 week. Stew can also be frozen in airtight container up to 3 months.

Makes 12 servings

vegetable

Asian Sugar Snap Pea Soup

- 2 tablespoons peanut or canola oil
- 4 to 5 new potatoes, coarsely chopped
- 2 green onions, chopped
- 1 medium carrot, peeled and sliced thin
- 1 stalk celery, sliced thin
- 1 leek, sliced thin
- 5 cups water
- 2 cups broccoli, washed and cut into florets
- 1 tablespoon lemon juice
- 1 tablespoon soy sauce
- 1 teaspoon ground coriander
- 1 teaspoon ground cumin
- 1 teaspoon prepared horseradish
- ⅛ teaspoon ground red pepper
- 1 cup fresh sugar snap peas, shelled rinsed and drained
- 4 cups cooked brown rice

1. Heat oil in skillet over medium heat until hot. Add potatoes, onions, carrot, celery and leek. Cook and stir 10 to 12 minutes or until vegetables begin to soften.

2. Transfer to 3½- to 4½-quart **CROCK-POT®** slow cooker. Add water, broccoli, lemon juice, soy sauce, coriander, cumin, horseradish and red pepper. Cover; cook on HIGH 2 to 3 hours or on LOW 5 to 6 hours.

3. Add sugar snap peas and stir again. Heat on HIGH until snap peas are crisp-tender, about 15 minutes. To serve, portion rice into 4 bowls. Ladle soup over rice and serve immediately.

Makes 4 servings

Middle Eastern Vegetable Stew

Combine all ingredients except rice in 4½-quart **CROCK-POT®** slow cooker. Cover; cook on LOW 5 to 5½ hours or until vegetables are tender. Serve over rice, if desired.

Makes 4 to 6 servings

1 tablespoon olive oil
3 cups sliced zucchini
2 cups peeled and cubed eggplant
2 cups peeled, quartered lengthwise and sliced sweet potatoes
1½ cups peeled, cubed butternut squash
1 can (28 ounces) crushed tomatoes in purée
1 cup canned chickpeas, drained and rinsed
½ cup raisins or currants
1½ teaspoons ground cinnamon
1 teaspoon grated orange peel
¾ to 1 teaspoon ground cumin
½ teaspoon salt
½ teaspoon paprika
¼ to ½ teaspoon ground red pepper
⅛ teaspoon ground cardamom
Hot cooked rice or couscous (optional)

A

Asian Sugar Snap Pea Soup 92
Autumn Apple and Squash Soup 84

B

Basic Stocks
    Slow Cooker Beef or Veal Stock............................8
    Slow Cooker Chicken Stock....................................9
    Slow Cooker Fish Stock 9
    Slow Cooker Vegetable Stock 7
Basil Oil 83

Beef and Lamb
    Beef, Lentil and Onion Soup..................................27
    Caramelized French Onion Soup..........................18
    Chuck and Stout Soup 16
    Curried Lamb and Swiss Chard Soup 28
    Hot Pot Noodle Soup..14
    Italian Beef and Barley Soup 24
    Lamb Stew 26
    Mushroom Soup 12
    Northwest Beef and Vegetable Soup 20
    Sweet and Sour Cabbage Soup 29
    Sweet and Sour Moroccan Lamb Soup 11
    Veggie Soup with Beef..29
    Wild Mushroom Beef Stew 22
Beef, Lentil and Onion Soup..27
Black Bean Soup 65

C

Cannellini Minestrone Soup 40
Caramelized French Onion Soup 18
Chicken and Chile Pepper Stew 44

Chicken and Turkey
    Cannellini Minestrone Soup 40
    Chicken and Chile Pepper Stew 44
    Chicken Miso Soup with Shiitake Mushrooms......31
    Chicken Tortilla Soup 38
    Curried Butternut Squash Soup 46
    Curried Chicken and Coconut Soup....................36
    Matzo Ball Soup..34
    Mediterranean Tomato, Oregano and Orzo Soup ...42
    Roasted Corn and Red Pepper Chowder..............47
    Southwestern Turkey Tenderloin Stew..................48
    Thai-Style Chicken and Pumpkin Soup................49
    Vietnamese Chicken Pho......................................32
Chicken Miso Soup with Shiitake Mushrooms 31
Chicken Tortilla Soup 38
Chuck and Stout Soup..16
Cioppino 79
Cod Fish Stew..78
Corn Chowder with Basil Oil..83
Country Sausage and Bean Stew................................58
Creamy Crab Bisque..81
Creamy Seafood Chowder..80
Curried Butternut Squash Soup..................................46
Curried Chicken and Coconut Soup..........................36
Curried Lamb and Swiss Chard Soup 28

G

Gumbo..62

H

Hot Pot Noodle Soup..14

I

Italian Beef and Barley Soup......................................24

L

Lamb Stew 26
Lentil Soup with Ham and Bacon 64
Lentil Stew over Couscous 90

M

Matzo Ball Soup..34
Matzo Balls..34
Mediterranean Tomato, Oregano and Orzo Soup.....42
Middle Eastern Vegetable Stew 93
Mushroom Soup..12